THE INTROVERT'S GUIDE TO LIFE

AN EXPLORATION OF SELF-DISCOVERY AND EMPOWERMENT

SUBHASH CHAUDHARY

Made with ♥ on the Notion Press Platform
www.notionpress.com

To all those who have ever felt misunderstood, misjudged, or like they don't fit in — this one's for you.

Contents

Foreword

The Introvert's Guide to Life is an essential guide for anyone who has ever felt like an outsider in a world that often celebrates extroversion. In this book, introverts will find solace and understanding of their unique gifts and learn new ways to thrive and grow.

It is easy to be overwhelmed by a world that is constantly seeking attention and approval. But the Introvert's Guide to Life provides a refreshing and empowering perspective on embracing the introverted lifestyle.

By embracing our unique qualities and finding ways to use them to our advantage, we can live a happier and more fulfilled life. This book is an invaluable resource, filled with practical advice and valuable insight on how to navigate life as an introvert. Whether you are looking to find a better balance between your introverted and extroverted sides, or simply want to learn how to be more confident and content in your own skin, this book is the perfect guide.

With its encouraging and supportive tone, The Introvert's Guide to Life is an essential tool for anyone who wants to understand and accept their introverted nature. And, more importantly, it will help you to recognize the beauty and power of your inner self.

Preface

The Introvert's Guide to Life is a comprehensive guide to the unique strengths and abilities that come with being an introvert. Drawing on research, personal experience, and anecdotes, this book offers insight into the life of an introvert and provides strategies to help them thrive in various aspects of life.

From exploring the psychological and neurological aspects of introversion to examining its implications in the workplace and social settings, this book provides introverts with the tools they need to understand and embrace their inner world. We will also cover how to build meaningful relationships, develop self-confidence, and maximize their potential.

This book is a must-read for introverts looking to make the most of their introversion and take control of their lives. Whether you're a student, a professional, or a parent, you'll find something in this book that will help you on your journey.

There's no need to be scared of your introversion. It's time to embrace it and use it to your advantage. The Introvert's Guide to Life is here to help you do just that.

Acknowledgements

First and foremost, I would like to thank my family for showing me unconditional love and support throughout the entire process of writing this book.

Special thanks to my editor and publisher for helping me bring this project to life.

I am also grateful to my mentor and friend who provided invaluable advice along the way.

Additionally, I would like to thank all of the introverts who have shared their stories with me. Your insight has been invaluable.

Finally, I am deeply thankful for the readers who have embraced this book and shared their feedback. Your support means the world to me.

Prologue

I'm an introvert. I'm the kind of person who prefers to stay in the background, who's more comfortable observing than being part of the action. I'm the one who prefers to get lost in my thoughts, and who finds solace in moments of silence. I'm the one who likes to take time to think things through before speaking or acting.

I know I'm not alone in this. There are many others out there, just like me, who identify as introverts. We may be quiet and shy on the outside, but inside we are often full of energy and creativity.

This book is for those who don't always fit in or stand out in a crowd. It's a guide to life for introverts and designed to help us make the most of who we are. We may not be the life of the party, but we can still lead fulfilling and meaningful lives.

With the help of this book, I hope to provide introverts with the tools and resources they need to discover their inner strength, find their purpose, and live life on their own terms.

CHAPTER ONE

UNDERSTANDING THE INTROVERT'S MINDSET

As an introvert, it is essential to understand your mindset and how it differs from that of an extrovert.

First, it is important to note that introversion is not a disorder but it is a personality trait. It is a way of being in a world that is unique to each individual. Introversion cannot be "cured" or "fixed." Instead, it is something that should be embraced and celebrated.

The introvert's mindset is characterized by a tendency to be more reserved, reflective, and independent. Introverts tend to prefer solo activities and quiet environments. They often enjoy solitary pursuits such as reading, writing, and creating art. They tend to be more thoughtful and introspective, and prefer to take their time to process their thoughts and feelings.

The introvert's mindset is also characterized by a need for personal space and quiet. Introverts often find it difficult to be in large groups or loud environments for extended periods of time. They need time alone to recharge and refocus.

The introvert's mindset also includes a preference for deep, meaningful conversation. Introverts tend to be more interested in having conversations that are thoughtful and meaningful. They tend to avoid small talk and prefer to focus on topics that are of interest to them.

Finally, the introvert's mindset is often characterized by a need for alone time. Introverts often need time to themselves to process their thoughts and feelings. They need time to reflect and to be in a quiet space in order to feel recharged.

Understanding the introvert's mindset is essential to living a life that is true to oneself. By embracing the introvert's mindset, introverts can find ways to make the most of their unique traits and talents.

CHAPTER TWO

Developing Self-Awareness as an Introvert

Self-awareness is a key component to living a fulfilling life as an introvert. As introverts, we can be prone to introspection and self-analysis, which can be beneficial if we take the time to understand ourselves better. To develop self-awareness as an introvert, it is important to recognize our strengths and weaknesses, as well as our needs and preferences.

One of the best ways for introverts to gain self-awareness is to reflect on our past experiences and identify patterns of behavior. It is also important to pay attention to our thoughts and feelings in different situations, as this can help us better understand ourselves. A journal can be a great tool for introverts to keep track of their thoughts and feelings in different situations.

The key to developing self-awareness as an introvert is to use our introspection to our advantage. We should take the time to really think about our needs and preferences, and how they affect our daily lives. Additionally, we should also be aware of our strengths and weaknesses, and use them to our advantage. This way, we can better understand ourselves and learn how to live a fulfilling life as an introvert.

In order to further develop self-awareness as an introvert, it is important to surround ourselves with people who accept and understand us. This can help us feel more comfortable in our own skin, and help us to better understand our needs and preferences. Additionally, it is also a good idea to take time out for ourselves and focus on our own needs and interests. This can help us to relax and recharge, as well as gain a better understanding of ourselves.

Overall, developing self-awareness as an introvert is an important part of living a fulfilling life. By taking the time to understand our needs and preferences, as well as our strengths and weaknesses, we can better understand ourselves and learn how to live a fulfilling life as an introvert.

CHAPTER THREE

Exploring the Benefits of Being an Introvert

As an introvert, you may sometimes feel overwhelmed by the hustle and bustle of the world around you. It can be difficult to find your place in a world that seems to demand extroversion. However, being an introvert can also be incredibly rewarding, and there are many benefits to embracing your introverted nature.

First and foremost, introversion allows you to think deeply and come up with creative solutions to problems. Introverts are often highly reflective and thoughtful individuals, which allows them to come up with innovative ideas that others may not have considered.

Additionally, introverts often have strong communication skills. Introverts tend to be comfortable with conversations that are more intimate and less noisy. This makes it easier for introverts to connect with others on a deeper level, and to communicate effectively in both professional and personal settings.

Furthermore, introverts can be highly productive. Introverts often have the ability to focus deeply on one task, which allows them to get more done in less time. Introverts also tend to be highly organized, which makes it easier for them to manage their workloads effectively.

Finally, introverts often have a strong resilience. Introverts tend to be comfortable with spending time alone, which can be a great source of strength when it comes to dealing with difficult situations. Introverts also tend to have strong emotional resilience, which helps them to remain calm and composed when faced with stress.

As an introvert, you have the potential to bring a lot of value to the world. Embracing your introverted nature can open up a world of opportunities and allow you to achieve great things. So, don't be afraid to explore the benefits of being an introvert.

CHAPTER FOUR

BUILDING SELF-CONFIDENCE AS AN INTROVERT

In today's world, the extrovert is often seen as the ideal, leaving those who are more introverted feeling that they are somehow at a disadvantage. But this is far from true; introverts have their own unique set of strengths, and it is possible to build self-confidence as an introvert.

The first step in building self-confidence as an introvert is to recognize and accept your introversion. This means understanding that being introverted is not a flaw or a weakness, but simply a personality trait. Once you have accepted your introversion, you can start to explore the ways in which it can be a strength.

For example, introverts often have a deep appreciation for learning and knowledge. This can give you great accomplishment and pride when you master a new skill or gain a better understanding of something. Furthermore, introverts are often great observers, which can give them a better understanding of the world around them. This can be a valuable asset in many situations.

In addition to recognizing and appreciating your introversion, it is also important to focus on developing your strengths. Introversion does not mean that you cannot be successful in the world. It simply means that you may need to approach things in a different way.

For example, if you are looking to build self-confidence in a professional setting, it is important to focus on developing the skills that will help you succeed in that environment. This could include working on your public speaking skills, networking, and researching topics related to your field. All of these activities can help to build your self-confidence.

Finally, it is important to remember that taking risks and trying new things is okay. Many introverts are hesitant to take risks, but this can be a great way to build self-confidence. Taking risks can help you learn new skills, meet new people, and gain new experiences. It can also help you to become more comfortable in unfamiliar situations.

Building self-confidence as an introvert is not easy, but it is possible. By recognizing and appreciating your introversion, developing your strengths, and taking risks, you can become a more confident and successful person.

CHAPTER FIVE

Finding Your Voice and Being Heard

Finding your voice and being heard as an introvert can be daunting, especially in a world that often seems geared towards extroverts. Whether in the workplace, social situations, or even just engaging in a conversation, it's important to find ways to make your voice heard and be confident in your opinions and ideas. This chapter will provide tips on how to do this, as well as strategies to help you gain more confidence in speaking up.

Making Your Voice Heard

1. Take Your Time: When faced with a situation where you need to speak up, don't rush it. Take a few moments to think about what you want to say and how you want to say it. This will allow you to organize your thoughts and ensure that you're conveying what you want most clearly and effectively as possible.

2. Prepare in Advance: If you know you'll be in a situation where you need to make your voice heard, take some time to think about what you want to say and how you want to say it. Writing your thoughts down beforehand can help you to organize your thoughts and give you more confidence when it comes time to speak.

3. Speak up with Confidence: Even if you're nervous or unsure, it's important to speak confidently. Make sure you speak in a clear and confident voice and keep your posture open and relaxed.

4. Use Visual Aids: If you're giving a presentation or speaking in a group setting, consider using visual aids such as charts, graphs, or images to help communicate your point. This can help to make your point clearer and easier to understand.

5. Ask Questions: Asking questions is a great way to show that you're engaged in the conversation and get clarification on points you don't understand. This is especially important in a group setting, as it will help ensure everyone is on the same page.

6. Listen to Others: It's important to remember to listen to others and respect their opinions, even if you don't agree with them. This will help ensure that everyone feels heard and create a more respectful and productive conversation overall.

7. Stay Positive: If you disagree with someone or express a different opinion, it's important to stay positive and focus on the issue rather than attacking the other person. This will help to ensure that the conversation remains constructive.

Conclusion

Finding your voice and being heard as an introvert can be difficult, but it is possible. Following the tips outlined above and being mindful of your own needs, you can find ways to make your voice heard and gain more confidence in speaking up. Remember to take your time, prepare in advance, and stay positive, and you'll be on your way to finding your voice and being heard.

CHAPTER SIX

Establishing and Maintaining Healthy Relationships

As an introvert, it can sometimes feel like our unique personality traits can be a barrier when it comes to forming and maintaining healthy relationships. We may feel like we don't fit in, or that our thoughts and opinions are not valued.

However, building and maintaining relationships with others is an important part of life, and introverts can be just as successful at it as extroverts. The key to establishing and maintaining healthy relationships as an introvert is to set boundaries, be honest, and open up at your own pace.

Here are some tips for establishing and maintaining healthy relationships as an introvert:

1. Take Time To Reflect: Introverts tend to think more deeply, and it's important to take the time to reflect on our feelings and thoughts before entering a relationship. This will help us stay true to ourselves and ensure that we are entering into the relationship for the right reasons.

2. Set Boundaries: It's important to set boundaries in all relationships, and it's particularly important for introverts. We tend to be more sensitive to energy and emotions, so it's important to ensure that we are not being taken advantage of or overwhelmed.

3. Be Honest: We can't form meaningful relationships without being honest about who we are and how we feel. If we are honest and open with

others, they will be more likely to trust and be open with us in return.

4. Take It Slow: Introverts often need more time to process things and open up. It's important to take things slow and allow yourself the time to get to know someone before committing to a deeper connection.

5. Listen and Communicate: As an introvert, it can be hard to express our feelings and thoughts. However, it's important to listen to others and communicate with them in order to build stronger relationships.

By following these tips, introverts can establish and maintain healthy relationships with others. By taking the time to get to know ourselves and others, setting boundaries, being honest, and taking things slow, we can develop meaningful relationships that will last a lifetime.

CHAPTER SEVEN

CREATING A HAPPY, BALANCED LIFE

As an introvert, it can be easy to forget to take care of yourself in the hustle and bustle of life. It is important to take some time out and create a balance in your life that will make you happy and content.

Start by taking some time out to assess your current situation. What are your priorities and goals? What are the things that make you happiest? What do you need to do to achieve a balanced life?

Focus on the things that make you happy and put those activities first. Schedule time for yourself each week to do something that is meaningful to you. Whether it is reading a book, going for a walk, listening to music, or engaging in a hobby, make sure to make time for those activities.

When it comes to working, it is important to stay on top of deadlines and to stay organized. Get into the habit of setting aside time for work and for yourself each day, and stick to it. Don't be afraid to delegate tasks to others if you need help.

Create healthy relationships that bring you joy. Surround yourself with people who appreciate and accept you for who you are. Be honest and open with your friends and family. Spend quality time with them and make sure to let them know how much you value them.

Finally, don't forget to take care of your body and mind. Eat healthy, get enough sleep, and exercise regularly. Make sure to take a break and relax when needed. Meditation and yoga can be great ways to reduce stress and can help you stay focused and calm.

Creating a balanced life is essential for introverts. Taking time to assess your current situation, focus on the activities that make you happy, and take care of your body and mind will help you lead a happier, more fulfilled life.

Conclusion

The Introvert's Guide to Life is a guide to living your life as an introvert. It has covered topics ranging from accepting your introversion to dealing with people and situations, to understanding your strengths and weaknesses. It has also provided tips on how to manage your energy, cultivate meaningful relationships, and find meaningful work.

Your journey as an introvert is an ongoing process of learning and growth. No matter what stage you're at in your journey, it's important to remember that you have the power to make your life meaningful and enjoyable. Don't let any preconceived notions of how an introvert should live their life limit you.

You can find success and fulfilment as an introvert, but it requires you to be true to yourself. You must learn to embrace your introversion, understand your unique gifts, and make conscious choices to help you succeed and thrive.

The Introvert's Guide to Life is meant to be a helpful resource to help you on your journey. Take the knowledge you have gained and use it to create a life that is uniquely yours.

9 798888 909135 6